Which season is it?

Bobbie Kalman

🍄 Crabtree
Publishing Company
www.crabtreebooks.com

Created by Bobbie Kalman

Author and Editor-in-Chief
Bobbie Kalman

Educational consultants
Elaine Hurst
Joan King
Jennifer King

Notes for adults
Jennifer King

Editors
Kathy Middleton
Crystal Sikkens

Design
Bobbie Kalman
Katherine Berti

Print and production coordinator
Katherine Berti

Prepress technician
Katherine Berti

Photo research
Bobbie Kalman

Photographs by Shutterstock

Library and Archives Canada Cataloguing in Publication

Kalman, Bobbie, 1947-
     Which season is it? / Bobbie Kalman.

(My world)
Issued also in electronic format.
ISBN 978-0-7787-9553-7 (bound).--ISBN 978-0-7787-9578-0 (pbk.)

     1. Seasons--Juvenile literature. I. Title. II. Series: My world
(St. Catharines, Ont.)

QB637.4.K34 2011   j508.2   C2010-907430-0

Library of Congress Cataloging-in-Publication Data

Kalman, Bobbie.
  Which season is it? / Bobbie Kalman.
      p. cm. -- (My world)
   ISBN 978-0-7787-9578-0 (pbk. : alk. paper) -- ISBN 978-0-7787-9553-7
(reinforced lib. bdg. : alk. paper) -- ISBN 978-1-4271-9660-6 (electronic
(pdf)
   1. Seasons--Juvenile literature. I. Title. II. Series.

   QB637.4.K35 2011
   508.2--dc22

                                                              2010047119

Crabtree Publishing Company

www.crabtreebooks.com   1-800-387-7650

Printed in China/022011/RG20101116

Copyright © **2011 CRABTREE PUBLISHING COMPANY**. All rights reserved. No part of this publication may be reproduced, stored in a retrieval system or be transmitted in any form or by any means, electronic, mechanical, photocopying, recording, or otherwise, without the prior written permission of Crabtree Publishing Company. In Canada: We acknowledge the financial support of the Government of Canada through the Canada Book Fund for our publishing activities.

Published in Canada
Crabtree Publishing
616 Welland Ave.
St. Catharines, Ontario
L2M 5V6

Published in the United States
Crabtree Publishing
PMB 59051
350 Fifth Avenue, 59th Floor
New York, New York 10118

Published in the United Kingdom
Crabtree Publishing
Maritime House
Basin Road North, Hove
BN41 1WR

Published in Australia
Crabtree Publishing
386 Mt. Alexander Rd.
Ascot Vale (Melbourne)
VIC 3032

Words to know

autumn

dry season

spring

summer

wet season

winter

Many places have four **seasons**.
Which season is it in each picture?
Snow falls in this season.
Flowers bloom in this season.

snow

flowers

The days are hot in this season.
The leaves fall in this season.

Winter is the season
when it snows.
It is cold outside.
I wear these clothes
to keep me warm.

hat

gloves

snowsuit

boots

I have fun in winter.
I love to ski!
I like making a snowman
with my family.

Spring is the season
when flowers bloom.
I like to wear flowers.

flowers

butterfly

I have fun in spring.
It is warm and sunny.
I play outside with my friends.

Summer is the hottest season of all!
I like to go swimming every day.

I have fun in summer.
What do you like to do in summer?

go inline
skating

ride a
skateboard

jump on
a ball

11

Autumn is the season when the leaves fall. That is why people call it "fall."

I have fun in autumn.
I like playing in autumn leaves.
I like making a hat from the leaves.

What do you do in each season?
Which season do you like the best?

winter

spring

summer

autumn (fall)

14

Did you know?

Some places have only two seasons.
In the **wet season**, it rains a lot.
In the **dry season**, it does not rain.
This girl is wet from rain.
Which season is it where she lives?

Notes for adults

Objectives
- to identify the seasons based on climate and activities
- to allow children to explore their experiences with the seasons

Questions before reading book
Write these frequently used words on the board: a, all, ball, day, do, each, fall, four, fun, go, have, hot, I, in, is, it, like, love, many, me, my, of, on, the, these, this, to, when, which, with, you

Bring in clothing worn in each season. Ask the children when they would wear each piece of clothing.
Example: "In which season would I wear this thick jacket?"
Guide children to the cover and title page. Ask them:
"Which seasons can you see on the front cover?"
"What is the boy dressed to do?"
"In which season do you see many flowers and butterflies?"
"In which season can you make a hat like the boy on the title page made?"

Questions after reading book
"What do you do in each season?"
"Which season do you like the best?"
"Which season do you like the least?"
"Why do you like or not like those seasons?"
"Which season is it now?" (Prompt the children to explain the weather, attire, and activities that go along with the current season.)

Activity: Match the seasons
Put up chart paper with a different season on each one. Have the children give vocabulary words from the book to match each season. Write down their words on each chart.

Seasonal wreaths
Set up four centers with a wreath at each center. Have the children glue to the wreaths small pictures of objects they have drawn that represent the seasons. Examples:
Summer: flowers, a sun, beach attire, beach toys
Winter: snowman, toboggan, snow sports
Fall: pumpkins, leaves, Halloween costumes
Spring: eggs, baby animals, flowers, butterflies

Extension
Read *What time is it?* to the children and explore with them different times, such as clock time, day and night, months, and years.
Guided reading: J

For teacher's guide, go to www.crabtreebooks.com/teachersguides